LOCOMOTIVES AT BR WORKSHOPS

Andrew Cole

AMBERLEY

First published 2017

Amberley Publishing
The Hill, Stroud
Gloucestershire, GL5 4EP

www.amberley-books.com

Copyright © Andrew Cole, 2017

The right of Andrew Cole to be identified as the Author of this work has been asserted in accordance with the Copyrights, Designs and Patents Act 1988.

ISBN 978 1 4456 7230 4 (print)
ISBN 978 1 4456 7231 1 (ebook)

All rights reserved. No part of this book may be reprinted or reproduced or utilised in any form or by any electronic, mechanical or other means, now known or hereafter invented, including photocopying and recording, or in any information storage or retrieval system, without the permission in writing from the Publishers.

British Library Cataloguing in Publication Data.
A catalogue record for this book is available from the British Library.

Origination by Amberley Publishing.
Printed in the UK.

Introduction

Welcome to my pictorial tribute to one of the unsung parts of British Rail – the workshops. British Rail Engineering Limited (BREL) came into being in 1969, and was formed to take control of the various workshops around the country.

When British Rail was formed in 1948, most of the former pre-nationalised companies had various workshops dotted around the country, some small and some large, that looked after their own fleets. Many of the smaller workshops were to close, with the majority of the work undertaken by the larger workshops.

These workshops undertook all manner of work for British Rail, from construction to classified and unclassified repairs and overhauls. Collision repairs were also undertaken, and even the scrapping of redundant locomotives was done virtually entirely in-house. The only part of this that changed significantly was the scrapping process, mainly due to the vast numbers of redundant wagons, carriages, units and locomotives that needed to be disposed of, with BR selling them to private contractors.

BREL was left with the major Works at Crewe, Derby, Doncaster, Eastleigh, Horwich, St Rollox (Glasgow), Swindon, and also the smaller works at Derby Litchurch Lane, Wolverton and York, although the latter three concentrated more on rolling stock and units compared to the others. As can be seen, there was roughly one works to every BR region.

The first of the big seven to close was Swindon in 1986, just after the GWR 150th celebrations. The announcement of the closure resulted in one of the saved 'Warships' being scrapped. This was followed soon after with the closure of Horwich Works. The next works to close was Derby in 1990, and very little remains of both sites today. Today the other three major workshops are still in use, although their size has dramatically decreased, both in workload and also in physical size. BREL was privatized in 1989, with some of the workshops being sold.

Crewe was sold to Adtranz, and has since been taken over by Bombardier. Some of the workshops – Doncaster, Eastleigh, Wolverton and St Rollox – continued to see use under the British Rail Maintenance Limited (BRML) banner. BRML was privatized in 1995, with the workshops being sold off.

Eastleigh Works eventually went through a management buyout, and became Wessex Traincare Ltd. This was eventually brought by Alstom, who closed it in 2006. Despite this, Arlington Services have reopened part of the works for overhauls. Doncaster was sold to Wabtec and it has since closed, with its famous 'Crimpsall' maintenance shed being demolished. St Rollox (Glasgow) has been through various owners since BRML; it was first sold to Babcock/Siemens, who then sold it on to Alstom, who in turn sold it to RailCare Ltd and, when they went into administration, the site passed to Knorr-Bremse Ltd.

This album intends to document some of the work undertaken by the different workshops, and although the book leans heavily on Crewe Works, there are also photos included from Derby, Doncaster, Eastleigh, and St Rollox, with a few also from Swindon and Horwich.

I hope you enjoy browsing through this book as much as I have enjoyed compiling it. It has certainly jogged some good memories for me, and going around Crewe Works on official permits every two months in the 1980s was certainly great fun.

No. 03060, 15 May 1983
No. 03060 (D2060) is seen parked on the reception sidings at Doncaster Works. This Class 03 would spend many years of operation on the Eastern Region, and be withdrawn at the end of 1982, arriving at Doncaster soon after. It would linger inside the Works for another couple of months, before being scrapped in July 1983.

No. 03069, 27 July 1980
No. 03069 (D2069) is also seen at Doncaster Works while undergoing engine repairs. This loco was still in service at the time, but was withdrawn at the end of 1983. No. 03069 was sold to Vic Berry, Leicester, and was used as a yard pilot until it was sold for preservation. It can be found today at the Vale of Berkeley Railway, Sharpness.

No. 03109, 22 February 1976

No. 03109 (D2109) stands condemned in a line of various other Class 03 locomotives at Doncaster Works. No. 03109 had been withdrawn in 1975 and would only last another two months, being scrapped in April 1976.

No. 03370, 15 May 1983

No. 03370 (D2370, Departmental 91) is seen standing condemned inside Doncaster Works. This loco was originally numbered Departmental 91 and was based at Cambridge, but was later renumbered D2370. It was withdrawn at the end of 1982, and was scrapped at Doncaster in July 1983.

No. 2991, 3 April 1976

No. 2991 is seen at Eastleigh Works carrying BR blue livery, but with the 'D' prefix removed. This loco was one of fourteen built by Ruston & Hornsby for use on the Southern Region, based around Southampton Docks. No. 2991 was withdrawn in 1973 and was used at Eastleigh Works as a stationary generator. It was eventually preserved and can still be found today working at Eastleigh Works.

No. 20005, 25 February 1984

No. 20005 (D8005) is seen is temporary storage at Crewe Works. The Class 20s were overhauled at Crewe, but not in large numbers, as Derby and St Rollox also overhauled the class. No. 20005 was stored for three months before re-entering service, and it would be scrapped by MC Metals, Glasgow, in 1990.

No. 20026, 29 October 1983

No. 20026 (D8026) is seen at Crewe Works, also in temporary storage. The loco shows signs of repairs being undertaken, and it would re-enter service two months later. No. 20026 would eventually be scrapped by MC Metals, Glasgow, in 1991.

No. 20050, 15 May 1983

No. 20050 (D8000) is seen condemned at Doncaster Works. This was the pioneer Class 20 built and had been withdrawn from service in 1980, finding its way to Doncaster Works for overhaul and repainting for the National Railway Museum.

No. 20061, 29 October 1983

No. 20061 (D8061) stands outside one of the test houses at Crewe Works following overhaul. There is a large traverser at Crewe, making locomotive movements around the Works easier. No. 20061 would be scrapped by MC Metals, Glasgow, in 1994.

No. 24006, 26 October 1980

No. 24006 (D5006) is seen part way through scrapping at St Rollox Works, Glasgow. This loco had been withdrawn five years earlier and was used as a re-railing exercise loco at Eastfield before it was sent to St Rollox for scrapping.

No. 24101, 22 February 1976
No. 24101 (D5101) is seen on the reception sidings at Doncaster Works along with classmate No. 24100. Both of these locomotives had already been withdrawn, and had been sent to Doncaster Works to be scrapped by May 1976.

No. 24132, 22 February 1976
No. 24132 (D5132) stands in the yard at Doncaster Works, complete with snowploughs and its tablet-catching recess, and still retains its headcode blinds. It had been withdrawn from Inverness at the start of the month and would only last for another couple of weeks, being scrapped in March 1976.

No. 25028, 25 May 1986
No. 25028 (D5178) stands condemned in the yard at St Rollox Works, Glasgow. This loco had been withdrawn six years earlier and would go on to be sold to Vic Berry, Leicester, for scrapping, which would take place in June 1987.

No. 25034, 11 February 1984
No. 25034 (D5184) is seen inside Derby Works undergoing repairs for fire damage, which has included having its bogies removed. No. 25034 was out of use for over six months before being reinstated to traffic. It would eventually be scrapped by Vic Berry, Leicester, in 1988.

No. 25062, 11 February 1984

No. 25062 (D5212) is seen in the yard at Derby Works awaiting final disposal. No. 25062 had been withdrawn at the end of 1982, and was sent to Swindon Works for scrapping, which was completed in 1985. This area of Derby Works was known as 'Klondyke' sidings.

No. 25220, 11 February 1984

No. 25220 (D7570) is seen also at Derby Works, awaiting final scrapping and showing signs of already being partially stripped. No. 25220 had been withdrawn from Crewe Depot in 1982 and was another loco sent to Swindon for final scrapping, this taking place in April 1985.

No. 26013, 14 September 1980

No. 26013 (D5313) is seen in storage at Crewe Works. This Scottish-based loco was stored at Crewe for approximately nine months before being sent back to Scotland, but would only last in service until 1982. No. 26013 was sold to Vic Berry for scrapping, which took place in 1987.

No. 26027, 3 September 1994

No. 26027 (D5327) stands condemned in the yard at Springburn Works, Glasgow. This loco had been the target of a preservation bid by the Bodmin & Wenford Railway, but the deal fell through, and it was sold to MC Metals for scrap instead. The MC Metals yard was adjacent to Springburn Works, and No. 26027 was moved next-door in January 1995 to be immediately scrapped.

No. 26030, 25 May 1986

No. 26030 (D5330) is seen inside St Rollox Works, Glasgow. This loco had been withdrawn the year previous, and was in the Works for stripping, despite the respectable appearance of the loco. It was later moved to Thornton Junction, and was scrapped there by Vic Berry in 1987.

No. 26033, 25 May 1986

No. 26033 (D5333) stands in the yard at St Rollox Works, having been condemned in 1985. The loco shows signs of parts removal already having taken place, and was another loco sent to Thornton Junction for scrapping by Vic Berry – this occurring in March 1987.

No. 26040, 25 May 1986
No. 26040 (D5340) is seen inside St Rollox Works, Glasgow, undergoing collision damage repairs, which included repanelling the front of the loco. No. 26040 would eventually be saved for preservation and can today be found at the Whitrope Heritage Railway.

No. 27008, 26 October 1980
No. 27008 (D5354) is seen on the reception sidings at St Rollox Works, Glasgow, outside the admin buildings. No. 27008 was based at Inverness at the time, and being the only major Works in Scotland, St Rollox undertook all repairs to the smaller Scottish-based locomotives. No. 27008 would be scrapped by MC Metals in 1987.

No. 27029, 25 May 1986
No. 27029 (D5376) stands condemned in the yard at St Rollox Works, Glasgow. This had been withdrawn at the start of the year, and like many other Scottish-based locomotives at the time that needed scrapping, it was sold to Vic Berry, and was moved to Thornton Junction for final processing, being scrapped in April 1987.

No. 27203, 6 June 1981
No. 27203 (D5393, 27121) is seen stored at Crewe Works – an unusual place for a Scottish-based Sulzer to be stored. It was later sent to Derby Works for repairs before being reinstated for service back at Eastfield. It would only last in service until September 1982, being withdrawn thereafter with collision damage.

No. 27203, 11 February 1984

No. 27203 (D5393, 27121) is seen condemned at Derby Works. It was withdrawn in 1982 following the collision damage it received after hitting 303018. No. 27203 would be scrapped by Vic Berry in 1986, but unusually it was scrapped at Etches Park, Derby, rather than Leicester.

No. 33007, 22 August 1987

No. 33007 (D6507) is seen at Eastleigh Works in the last stages of dismantling. This loco was withdrawn following collision damage it received at Chatham Dockyard. All of the main British Rail workshops dismantled locos, until numbers were so great that BR turned to private scrapyards.

No. 33023, 3 April 1976

No. 33023 (D6541) is seen inside the engine test house at Eastleigh Works following main overhaul. The loco gleams in a new coat of BR blue livery. No. 33023 was withdrawn and used as a source of spares for the small DRS fleet, and was finally scrapped by European Metal Recycling, Kingsbury, in 2005.

No. D7029, 8 June 1980

D7029 is seen stabled on one of the turntable roads at Swindon Works. This Hymek had been returned to original condition and was preserved. It can currently be found at Kidderminster on the Severn Valley Railway. Swindon Works was to close in 1986.

No. 37009, 25 February 1984

No. 37009 (D6709, 37340) leads a line of other Class 37s inside Crewe Works. Crewe was to undertake a major rebuilding programme on the class 37s, with a large number being refurbished. No. 37009 would not enter the refurbishment process and was eventually preserved at the Great Central Railway, Ruddington.

No. 37011, 10 May 1986

No. 37011 (D6711) is seen inside Crewe Works undergoing overhaul. This Class 37 was a Scottish-allocated loco at the time, and carries a headlight and Eastfield Scottie dog logo. No. 37011 would be withdrawn in 1987 with collision damage, before coming back to Crewe for stripping, and being sold to Rollason's of Wellington for final scrapping.

No. 37012, 10 May 1986

No. 37012 (D6712) looks superb standing in the reception roads at Crewe Works. 37012 carries the name *Loch Rannock*, and also large logo livery, complete with Eastfield Scottie dog. This was another Class 37 that never made the refurbishment programme, being scrapped at Brush, Loughborough, in 2002.

No. 37016, 25 January 1986

No. 37016 (D6716, 37706) stands on the reception roads at Crewe Works. There were many Class 37s on Crewe Works at this time, with the refurbishment programme in full swing. No. 37016 would enter the programme, but would not be completed until December 1987, emerging as No. 37706.

No. 37020, 17 August 1986

No. 37020 (D6720, 37702) is seen inside Crewe Works, having been completely stripped down and ready for refurbishing. The level of work undertaken was huge. No. 37020 would emerge as No. 37702 and, along with the other freight conversions, it would have its main generator changed for an alternator, while also having ballast weights added.

No. 37026, 22 March 1986

No. 37026 (D6726, 37320) is seen inside the paint shop at Crewe Works. This Scottish-based Class 37 carries the name *Loch Awe*, and when the painters had finished with No. 37026, it would emerge carrying a fresh coat of large logo livery. No. 37026 would be scrapped by EWS at Wigan CRDC in 2000.

No. 37038, 15 May 1983

No. 37038 (D6738) is seen in near original condition at Doncaster Works. No. 37038 still retains connecting doors, black headcode panels, and a bufferbeam skirt. Doncaster undertook a lot of the repair work on English Electric locomotives, but the Class 37s would start to have the work done by Crewe. No. 37038 is still in service today with DRS.

No. 37042, 22 March 1986

No. 37042 (D6742) stands in the reception roads at Crewe Works. No. 37042 carries an unofficial white stripe, and also a Thornaby white Kingfisher depot sticker. No. 37042 would be preserved, and can be found at the Eden Valley Railway.

No. 37044, 28 July 1984
No. 37044 (D6744, 37710) is seen outside the test house at Doncaster Works during the open day in 1984. No. 37044 would later visit Crewe Works to be refurbished, emerging as No. 37710.

No. 37062, 18 March 1990
No. 37062 (D6762) stands condemned inside Doncaster Works, showing signs of the collision damage it received that resulted in its withdrawal. The loco was in the Works for stripping of every reusable part, and it was then sent to Vic Berry, Leicester, the following month for final scrapping.

No. 37067, 17 August 1986

No. 37067 (D6767, 37703) is seen inside Crewe Works at the start of its refurbishment. The loco would be in Crewe for another five months, emerging as No. 37703 in January 1987. This loco would find work in Spain as L25, and would be preserved at the Bo'ness & Kinneil Railway.

No. 37091, 25 January 1986

No. 37091 (D6791, 37358) is seen having not long arrived at Crewe Works for repairs. At this time there were normally over 100 locos on Crewe Works undergoing repairs, overhaul, refurbishment, or awaiting scrapping. No. 37091 would be renumbered 37358, and would be scrapped by T. J. Thomson, Stockton, in 2007.

No. 37095, 27 October 1984
No. 37095 (D6795) gleams on the reception roads at Crewe Works. No. 37095 had been through for overhaul, and at this stage was either awaiting the finishing touches, or had already been for a test run. The Crewe Works test train was formed of a rake of carriages and was used for a run on the North Wales coast.

No. 37133, 17 August 1986
No. 37133 (D6833) is seen at Crewe Works having just arrived for overhaul. This was allocated to Eastfield at the time, and the bigger Scottish diesels visited either Crewe or Doncaster for overhaul or repairs, with St Rollox concentrating on the smaller Sulzer locos. No. 37133 would be scrapped at Carnforth in 2004.

No. 37138, 6 June 1981

No. 37138 (D6838, 025032) is seen at Crewe Works during the 1981 open day. This loco lead a fairly uneventful life, until it was chosen by EWS to have most of the bodyside and roof cut away, and it acted as an engine transporter at Toton, gaining the departmental number 025032 in the process.

No. 37139, 23 November 1985

No. 37139 (D6839) is seen on the reception roads at Crewe Works following collision damage repairs. The one end of the loco has been repaired, and painted in primer, and it was just waiting a visit to the paint shop to finish the repair. No. 37139 would be scrapped by T. J. Thomson, Stockton, in 2004.

No. 37196, 27 October 1984

No. 37196 (D6896) is seen at Crewe Works having arrived for overhaul. This was just before the refurbishment programme started, and No. 37196 was never chosen for the work. No. 37196 was allocated to Eastfield at the time, but upon release from Crewe, it would be transferred to Cardiff Canton. No. 37196 would eventually be scrapped by C. F. Booth, Rotherham, in 2009.

No. 37221, 25 February 1984

No. 37221 (D6921) stands outside the test area at Crewe Works following overhaul. This was one of the last parts of the overhaul, as it had already been repainted, and following testing it would have a quick test run, before being released back to traffic. No. 37221 was scrapped by C. F. Booth, Rotherham, in 2009.

No. 37260, 18 March 1990

No. 37260 (D6960) is seen in the condemned sidings at Doncaster Works. Despite carrying large logo livery, this loco was withdrawn following fire damage, and would eventually find its way to MC Metals, Glasgow, for scrapping in September 1991. No. 37260 formerly carried the name *Radio Highland*.

No. 37263, 25 February 1984

No. 37263 (D6963) stands in the reception sidings at Crewe having arrived for overhaul. The Class 37 stands in front of a pair of Class 40s that were in Works for scrapping. No. 37263 would eventually find its way into preservation, and is currently pending a move to the Telford Steam Railway.

No. 37418, 23 November 1985

No. 37418 (D6971, 37271) is seen at Crewe Works having just been refurbished, and rebuilt from No. 37271. The loco was waiting to be released to Inverness, for passenger workings in the Highlands of Scotland. The Class 37s looked superb in this livery, and No. 37418 was eventually preserved at the East Lancashire Railway.

No. 37419, 23 November 1985

No. 37419 (D6991, 37291) is seen parked outside the main overhaul shop at Crewe Works, having just been refurbished and rebuilt from No. 37291. There were thirty-one Class 37/4s rebuilt for passenger workings in Scotland and South Wales. No. 37419 is still in service today, working for DRS.

No. 37421, 23 November 1985

No. 37421 (D6967, 37267) is seen at Crewe undergoing final testing following refurbishment from No. 37267. The Class 37/4 refurbishments were similar to the freight conversions, except that they were fitted with electric train heating, and they never received the extra ballast weights for adhesion. No. 37421 is currently operated by Colas on Network Rail test trains.

No. 37424, 10 July 1994

No. 37424 (D6979, 37279) is seen at Doncaster Works with collision damage. No. 37424 carries the name *Isle of Mull*, but these would be removed when the loco departed. No. 37424 is still in use today with DRS, but it carries the number 37558.

No. 37425, 22 March 1986

No. 37425 (D6992, 37292) is seen outside Crewe Works during the final testing before being released to Eastfield Depot for passenger workings in Scotland. No. 37425 had been rebuilt from No. 37292, and it is still in use today with DRS.

No. 37427, 25 January 1986

No. 37427 (D6988, 37288) is seen at Crewe Works following refurbishment work, having been rebuilt from No. 37288. This was one of the Cardiff Canton-allocated Class 37/4s, and it would be released from Crewe just a couple of weeks later. No. 37427 would eventually be scrapped by C. F. Booth, Rotherham, in 2013.

No. 37431, 22 March 1986

No. 37431 (D6972, 37272) is seen inside the paint shop at Crewe Works, getting ready to receive a coat of large logo livery. This was the final Class 37/4 rebuild, and it had been rebuilt from No. 37272. No. 37431 was stored at Springburn Works in 1996, and was reinstated for a couple of months, before finally being withdrawn and stripped for spares at Wigan CRDC. It was eventually scrapped in 2000.

No. 37506, 22 March 1986

No. 37506 (D6707, 37007, 37604) is seen outside one of the test houses at Crewe Works following refurbishment. This was rebuilt from 37007 and was repainted into original Railfreight livery. It would get rebuilt again and is still in use today with DRS, but carries the number 37604.

No. 37508, 10 May 1986

No. 37508 (D6790, 37090, 37606) is seen on the reception roads at Crewe Works having already been out for a test run following refurbishment. It had been rebuilt from No. 37090, and would be another to be rebuilt for EPS, this time being renumbered 37606.

No. 37509, 17 August 1986

No. 37509 (D6793, 37093) is seen undergoing testing at Crewe Works following refurbishment. The level of work involved was considerable on the freight conversions, and this included the removal of the redundant headcode boxes, replacing them with marker lights. No. 37509 was rebuilt from No. 37093, and it would eventually be scrapped at Cardiff Canton in 2005.

No. 37697, 10 May 1986

No. 37697 (D6943, 37243) stands on the departure roads at Crewe Works, ready to be dispatched back to Cardiff Canton after being rebuilt from No. 37243. This loco would eventually be scrapped by C. F. Booth, Rotherham, in 2006.

No. 37698, 25 January 1986

No. 37698 (D6946, 37246) is seen undergoing brake testing outside the main repair shed at Crewe Works. The loco was on its final stages of testing following refurbishment work, and looks superb carrying original Railfreight livery. It was rebuilt from No. 37246 and would be scrapped by C. F. Booth, Rotherham, in 2010.

No. 37905, 20 May 1990

No. 37905 (D6836, 37136) is seen on display at Doncaster Works open day 1990. This loco had been rebuilt from No. 37136 and was one of just two Class 37s fitted with Ruston RK270T engines. Both were preserved, and No. 37905 carries the name *Vulcan Enterprise*.

No. 40003, 15 May 1983

No. 40003 (D203) stands forlornly in the scrap lines at Doncaster Works. At this time, withdrawals of the class were gathering pace, and No. 40003 had been withdrawn in September 1982. It would be scrapped at Doncaster in January 1984.

No. 40004, 25 January 1986

No. 40004 (D204) is seen standing on the scrap lines at Crewe Works. Crewe was responsible for scrapping many of these huge locomotives, with No. 40004 being scrapped in September 1986.

No. 40006, 2 April 1983

No. 40006 (D206) is seen on the reception roads at Crewe Works. This loco had arrived as it had been withdrawn from service, and had been sent to Crewe for scrapping. These locomotives seemed to spend many months at Crewe being stripped, with No. 40006 being scrapped in August 1984.

No. 40008, 25 February 1984

No. 40008 (D208) stands among many other withdrawn Class 40s outside the melt shop at Crewe Works. Crewe used to scrap their withdrawn locomotives in a massive shed, rather than outdoors like many of the other BREL Works. No. 40008 would linger for another four years before being scrapped.

No. 40013, 25 February 1984

No. 40013 (D213) is seen on the reception roads at Crewe Works. Despite being in the Works, this loco was still in active service, and it wouldn't be withdrawn until 1985. No. 40013 was one of the lucky Class 40s, being preserved. No. 40013 once carried the name *Andania*.

No. 40020, 27 October 1984

No. 40020 (D220) is seen at Crewe Works looking in a very weather-worn condition. When new, No. 40020 was named *Franconia*, and by the time of this photo, it had been withdrawn for two years. It would eventually be scrapped at Crewe in 1987.

No. 40044, 23 November 1985

No. 40044 (D244) is seen in the scrap lines at Crewe Works. This loco had been badly damaged when it derailed at Chinley in 1978, but it was repaired and returned to service. It would eventually be scrapped at Crewe in 1988.

No. 40104, 26 July 1981
No. 40104 (D304) is seen at Crewe Works, having arrived for derailment repairs. No. 40104 would last in service until 1985, but would return to Crewe Works for scrapping, which happened in 1988.

No. 40115, 2 June 1984
No. 40115 (D315) is seen in the scrap lines at Crewe Works. The large building in the background is the melt shop, where Crewe used to dismantle the scrap locomotives. Today, this area of the Works had been redeveloped as a supermarket.

No. 40131, 27 October 1984

No. 40131 (D331) is seen inside the melt shop at Crewe Works part-way through being dismantled. Crewe scrapped many of these huge locomotives, and No. 40131 was finally completely scrapped during the following month.

No. 40132, 13 April 1985

No. 40132 (D332) stands in the scrap lines at Derby Works. This heavily stripped loco was withdrawn three years earlier, and would eventually be sold to Vic Berry of Leicester for final scrapping, which took place on 1987. Note how the pony wheels have already been removed.

No. 40138, 2 April 1983

No. 40138 (D338) is seen inside Crewe Works. This loco had arrived from Doncaster Works for scrapping, which Crewe completed in February 1984.

No. 40138, 29 October 1983

No. 40138 (D338) stands outside the melt shop at Crewe Works awaiting scrapping. It would be moved into the melt shop just four months later, being scrapped in February 1984. Of the three different front-end designs, this is my favourite.

No. 40142, 6 June 1981

No. 40142 (D342) stands condemned at Crewe Works during the open day in 1981. This had been withdrawn following collision damage, and would be scrapped at Crewe in 1983.

No. 40143, 22 March 1986

No. 40143 (D343) stands condemned outside the melt shop at Crewe Works among many other withdrawn Class 40s. No. 40143 was withdrawn in February 1985 and would be scrapped in October 1986. Today, none of this area of the Works survives, with it being redeveloped.

No. 40160, 23 November 1985

No. 40160 (D360) is seen on the reception roads at Crewe Works. This loco had arrived for scrapping, which Crewe completed in 1987. Crewe continued scrapping locos up until 1988, when the work was handed over to private contractors.

No. 40163, 13 April 1985

No. 40163 (D363) contemplates its future at Derby Works. Derby had stopped scrapping locomotives by this time, and the locomotives that were in storage were sold on to private contractors, with No. 40163 being sold to Vic Berry of Leicester, and No. 40163 was scrapped in 1987.

No. 40166, 23 May 1982

No. 40166 (D366) is seen on the reception roads at Crewe Works. This had been withdrawn earlier in the year, and it would be scrapped at Crewe in June 1983. Of note is the fact that No. 40166 retained its headcode blinds until it was scrapped.

No. 40177, 25 January 1986

No. 40177 (D377) is seen inside the melt shop part way through being dismantled. This was always one of my favourite parts of the Works to visit, as it would be home to one of these massive locomotives being scrapped. No. 40177 would linger for another four months.

No. 40183, 13 January 1980

No. 40183 (D383) is seen in the sunshine at Crewe Works positively gleaming following overhaul. The loco is seen undergoing final testing before being released back to Healey Mills. It would only be in service for another three years.

No. 40183, 29 October 1983

No. 40183 (D383) is seen condemned inside Crewe Works. Just three years separates the two photographs of No. 40183, but shows how work-stained these locomotives used to be. At this time Crewe was home to many withdrawn Class 40s, with the Works slow to dismantle them. No. 40183 would last for another three years, before being scrapped in 1986.

No. D818, 8 June 1980

D818 *Glory* is seen parked outside Swindon Works undergoing a repaint back into British Railways green livery. This loco, like the rest of the Warships, had been withdrawn for many years and was put on static display at Swindon. D818 would be hastily scrapped in 1985 following the decision to close the Works.

No. D832, 8 February 1981

D832 is seen at Horwich Works carrying British Railways green livery. This loco, along with two Westerns, had been on display for the open day of 1980, and has had its *Onslaught* nameplate temporarily removed. Horwich Works was mainly responsible for carriage and unit repairs.

No. 45041, 13 April 1985
No. 45041 (D53) is seen inside Derby Works undergoing a heavy overhaul, which has included the removal of the bogies and most of the front end. No. 45041 would eventually be preserved, and today can be found at the Great Central Railway. No. 45041 has had its *Royal Tank Regiment* name removed.

No. 4505, 27 October 1984
No. 45053 (D76) is seen in the scrap lines at Crewe Works. This split headcode Class 45 had been withdrawn as long ago as 1981, and had originally been stored at Swindon Works before moving to Crewe. It would be scrapped by a private contractor at Crewe in 1988, being the only 'Peak' to be scrapped at Crewe.

No. 45055, 13 April 1985

No. 45055 (D84) *Royal Corps of Transport* is seen in the scrap lines at Derby Works. This loco had been withdrawn a couple of days earlier, and would be another locomotive to be sold from Derby to Vic Berry, Leicester, who scrapped it in 1986.

No. 45076, 29 October 1983

No. 45076 (D134) stands outside Crewe Works undergoing testing following overhaul. Crewe outshopped a few Class 45s during this time, although most of the Class 45 overhauls were completed by Derby Works. No. 45076 would be scrapped by MC Metals, Glasgow, in 1994.

No. 45134, 2 April 1983

No. 45134 (D126) stands on the departure roads at Crewe Works following overhaul, including a repaint in BR blue livery. No. 45134 would have another three years of revenue-earning service ahead of it, before being withdrawn in 1986. It was scrapped by MC Metals, Glasgow, in 1994.

No. 47005, 22 March 1986

No. 47005 (D1526) is seen on the reception roads at Crewe Works having arrived for overhaul. No. 7005 looks good with a black headcode panel, and was allocated to Gateshead at the time. No. 47005 would be scrapped by Booth Roe Metals, Rotherham, in 1994.

No. 47017, 25 January 1986
No. 47017 (D1570) stands at Crewe Works, not long after arriving for repairs. This was a Scottish-based loco at the time and Crewe undertook most of the repairs to the Class 47 fleet during this period, including the Scottish locos. No. 47017 was scrapped by Booth Roe Metals, Rotherham, in 1992.

No. 47018, 27 October 1984
No. 47018 (D1572) is seen at Crewe Works having recently arrived for repairs. The locomotive's batteries have still yet to be removed, this being one of the first jobs, as well as draining the fuel tanks. This was another Scottish-based loco at the time, and would be scrapped by Coopers Metals, Attercliffe, in 1994.

No. 47068, 23 November 1985
No. 47068 (D1652, 47632, 47848) is seen outside the main repair shed at Crewe Works, undergoing testing. This loco was chalked up as No. 47068, but it has already had its new ETH equipment fitted, so it should actually be No. 47632. This loco is still in use today with Rail Operations Group, as No. 47848.

No. 47069, 23 November 1985
No. 47069 (D1653, 47638, 47845, 57301) is seen on the arrival roads at Crewe Works. This had arrived for conversion to No. 47638, and would depart with ETH equipment and a coat of large logo livery. This loco is still in use today with DRS, having been rebuilt as No. 57301.

No. 47111, 25 February 1984

No. 47111 (D1699) is seen on the arrival roads at Crewe Works having arrived for repairs. This loco would be involved in a serious collision at Preston in 1986, which resulted in its withdrawal. It would be towed to Cardiff Canton for stripping, and was scrapped there in 1987.

No. 47118, 25 February 1984

No. 47118 (D1706) looks resplendent at Crewe Works, having been overhauled. This was originally designated as one of the Class 48s, but was converted back to a Class 47, having had its French-built Sulzer engine replaced. No. 47118 was scrapped at Doncaster Depot by private contractor in 1995.

No. 47119, 13 December 1986
No. 47119 (D1708) is seen undergoing brake testing outside the main repair shed at Crewe Works. No. 47119 had received a coat of original Railfreight livery, and was withdrawn from service following collision damage it received at Billingham. It was scrapped at Frodingham Depot by private contractor in 1995.

No. 47157, 2 April 1983
No. 47157 (D1750) is seen on the arrival roads at Crewe Works. When freshly overhauled locomotives were seen on the arrival roads, it meant that they had been out for a test run, and had returned for rectification work. No. 47157 would be scrapped by Booth Roe Metals, Rotherham, in 2004.

No. 47162, 2 April 1983

No. 47162 (D1756) stands at Crewe Works carrying BR blue livery. This was one of the first Class 47s that was withdrawn as being life-expired, and was stripped for spare parts for other members of the class, before being scrapped at Crewe Works in 1987.

No. 47167, 13 January 1980

No. 47167 (D1762, 47580, 47732) *County of Essex* is seen at Crewe Works, having been stripped for conversion to No. 47580. This was fitted with ETH equipment for passenger workings out of London Liverpool Street, and was eventually preserved.

Locomotives at BR Workshops 55

No. 47184, 9 November 1980

No. 47184 (D1779, 47585, 47757) is seen at Crewe Works having been stripped ready for conversion to ETH locomotive No. 47585. This was another Class 47 that was allocated to Stratford for passenger workings out of London Liverpool Street, and it would finally be scrapped as No. 47757 by T. J. Thomson, Stockton, in 2004.

No. 47222, 2 April 1983

No. 47222 (D1872) is seen having just arrived at Crewe Works for overhaul. This was based at Immingham at the time and carried the name *Appleby Frodingham*. No. 47222 would be scrapped by C. F. Booth, Rotherham, in 1998, following the collision damage it received at Wembley Yard

No. 47275, 17 August 1986
No. 47275 (D1977) is seen in storage at Crewe Works, having suffered damage to its main generator, with holes in the roof and bodyside by the BR double arrow. This damage proved terminal, and the loco was scrapped by C. F. Booth, Rotherham, in 1989.

No. 47291, 20 May 1990
No. 47291 (D1993) stands at Doncaster Works having arrived for overhaul. The loco carries large logo livery, and *The Port of Felixstowe* nameplates. Upon release from Doncaster, No. 47291 would be painted in Railfreight Speedlink livery. It would be scrapped, having suffered collision damage, by C. F. Booth, Rotherham, in 2004.

No. 47313, 27 October 1984

No. 47313 (D1794) is seen outside the main repair shed at Crewe Works undergoing final testing before being released back to traffic. The loco has already been repainted into BR blue livery, and would be released back to Thornaby Depot. No. 47313 was scrapped by European Metal Recycling, Kingsbury, in 2007.

No. 47368, 13 December 1986

No. 47368 (D1887) is seen ready to depart from Crewe Works following overhaul and repaint into original Railfreight livery. This loco would end up in the Crewe Railfreight Petroleum pool, named *Neritidae*, and is currently in long-term storage at Carnforth.

No. 47405, 2 April 1983

No. 47405 (D1504) is seen at Crewe Works having arrived for overhaul. This was one of the original generator Class 47s, and along with the others was based at Gateshead at the time. No. 47405 carries the name *Northumbria*, and it would be scrapped at Crewe Works in 1988 by private contractor.

No. 47406, 23 November 1985

No. 47406 (D1505) *Rail Riders* is seen at Crewe Works carrying InterCity livery. This was the only member of the original generator Class 47s to receive this livery. No. 47406 would be scrapped at Frodingham Depot by private contractor in 1995.

No. 47409, 23 November 1985
No. 47409 (D1508) *David Lloyd George* is seen on the arrival roads at Crewe Works. At this time you could almost guarantee seeing some of the generator Class 47s at Crewe, as some of the members were nearing the end of their working lives. No. 47409 was scrapped following fire damage by Vic Berry, Leicester, in 1989.

No. 47449, 22 March 1986
No. 47449 (D1566) is seen at Crewe Works awaiting dispatch following overhaul. The work included a repaint into large logo livery, which was standard at the time. No. 47449 would eventually be preserved, and can today be found at the Llangollen Railway.

No. 47458, 27 October 1984

No. 47458 (D1578) is seen on the arrival roads at Crewe Works, having arrived with severe collision damage. This was based at Stratford at the time, and as such has a silver roof. No. 47458 would be repaired and returned to service, but was eventually scrapped by Booth Roe Metals, Rotherham, in 1996.

No. 47460, 22 March 1986

No. 47460 (D1580) stands at Crewe Works having arrived for overhaul. This was allocated to Inverness at the time, and shows that Crewe overhauled nearly all the Class 47s, from the length and breadth of the country. No. 47460 was scrapped by Booth Roe Metals, Rotherham, in 1994. No. 47460 carries large logo livery and looks superb with a full set of miniature snowploughs.

No. 47464, 13 December 1986

No. 47464 (D1587) is seen having arrived at Crewe Works with severe collision damage. No. 47464 received this damage when it collided with No. 37416 at Elgin; the damage was to prove terminal, with No. 47464 being scrapped at Crewe Works in 1987.

No. 47469, 10 May 1986

No. 47469 (D1595) is seen partway through an overhaul inside Crewe Works. The loco is also partway through a repaint into InterCity Scotrail livery – a variation that was only carried by a handful of Class 47s. No. 47469 carries the name *Glasgow Chamber of Commerce*, and was withdrawn with severe collision damage, being scrapped by MC Metals, Glasgow, in 1989.

No. 47470, 25 February 1984

No. 47470 (D1596) *University of Edinburgh* is seen at Crewe Works, having arrived with severe collision damage. The Class 47s seemed to have their fair share of collisions, and Crewe always seemed able to repair most of them. No. 47470 would eventually be scrapped at Crewe Works in 1995 by private contractor.

No. 47473, 14 February 1987

No. 47473 (D1601) is another Class 47 to arrive at Crewe Works with collision damage. It too would be repaired and released back to traffic to Bescot Depot. This loco would end up being stored at Crewe Works, and was scrapped there in 1998 by private contractor.

No. 47522, 18 March 1990

No. 47522 (D1105) *Doncaster Enterprise* is seen in storage at Doncaster Works after receiving collision damage at Dover. This loco was involved in a very serious collision at Forteviot, which resulted in the loco being completely rebuilt from the frames upwards in 1982.

No. 47526, 22 March 1986

No. 47526 (D1109) is seen outside one of the test houses at Crewe Works. This loco has just been through the Works for overhaul and is nearly ready for a return to traffic. Behind the loco can be seen the traversa, which at Crewe has many roads leading off it. Today No. 47526 is stored at Carnforth for spares.

No. 47535, 29 October 1983

No. 47535 (D1649) is seen inside Crewe Works undergoing unclassified collision damage repairs. This loco was involved in a serious collision at Luton station, which resulted in the need for a new cab. No. 47535 carries the name *University of Leicester*, and was eventually scrapped at Old Oak Common Depot by private contractor in 2004.

No. 47541, 22 March 1986

No. 47541 (D1755, 47773) is seen on the arrival roads at Crewe Works. Crewe was a regular host to the Scottish-based Class 47s, and they were always eagerly sought after. No. 47541 carries the name *The Queen Mother*, and looks superb in large logo livery, complete with snowploughs and black headcode panel. No. 47541 is still in use today, numbered 47773 and working for Vintage Trains.

No. 47557, 9 March 1980
No. 47557 (D1591, 47024, 47721) is seen at Crewe Works having been fully overhauled, and converted from No. 47024. At this time British Rail identified a need for a fleet of ETH fitted Class 47s, and Crewe was entrusted with the conversion work. No. 47557 was eventually scrapped by European Metal Recycling, Kingsbury, in 2007 while carrying the number 47721.

No. 47578, 27 October 1984
No. 47578 (D1776, 47181, 47776) is seen inside Crewe Works undergoing repairs to collision damage. The damage is at the other end of the loco, and it is seen half-way through being repainted in standard BR blue livery. This loco is still intact today, being housed at Carnforth.

No. 47602, 29 October 1983

No. 47602 (D1780, 47185, 47824, 47782) is seen inside the paint shop at Crewe Works having been painted in standard BR blue livery. The paint shop at Crewe was quite spacious and could house a good number of locos. No. 47602 would go on to be renumbered 47824 and then 47782, and was scrapped by T. J. Thomson, Stockton, in 2007.

No. 47612, 13 December 1986

No. 47612 (D1665, 47080, 47638, 47779) is seen standing outside the main repair shed at the Crewe Works, having been through for overhaul, which included a repaint into InterCity livery. No. 47612 carries the name *Titan* and was one of the original Western Region-named Class 47s.

No. 47615, 2 June 1984

No. 47615 (D1929, 47252, 47747) is seen at Crewe Works undergoing air brake testing before being released back to traffic. The loco had been in the Works for conversion from No. 47252, and was fitted with ETH equipment. No. 47615 would go on to be renumbered 47747, and as such was scrapped by C. F. Booth, Rotherham, in 2013.

No. 47617, 17 August 1986

No. 47617 (D1742, 47149, 47677) stands on the arrival roads at Crewe Works having arrived for overhaul. This was based at Eastfield at the time, and as such, carries a Scottie dog logo, but it's not in the usual position of under the nameplate. No. 47617 carries the name *University of Stirling*, and it would go on to be renumbered 47677 for Scottish sleeper trains. It was scrapped by Booth Roe Metals, Rotherham, in 1998.

No. 47631, 23 November 1985

No. 47631 (D1643, 47059, 47765) is seen on the departure roads at Crewe Works, having been converted from No. 47059. The quality of paint finish that Crewe used to do was superb, and today No. 47631 has been preserved at the Great Central Railway, Ruddington, carrying the number 47765.

No. 47633, 1 May 1993

No. 47633 (D1668, 47083) is seen on the scrap lines at Springburn Works, Glasgow. This was converted from No. 47083, and had a short life as an ETH locomotive of just five years' service, being withdrawn in 1990. It would be shunted next door into the premises of MC Metals for scrapping, which was completed in 1994.

No. 47637, 25 January 1986
No. 47637 (D1976, 47274, 47826) is seen outside one of the test houses at Crewe Works. This had been converted from No. 47274, and is painted in InterCity ScotRail livery. There were only a handful of Class 47s painted in this livery with ScotRail branding. No. 47637 would go on to be renumbered 47826, and is still in service today with West Coast Railways.

No. 47646, 22 March 1986
No. 47646 (D1658, 47074, 47852) is seen undergoing brake testing outside the main repair shed at Crewe Works. This loco had entered the Works as No. 47074, and emerged having been fitted with ETH equipment, renumbered to 47646. This would be scrapped, carrying the number 47852, by Booth Roe Metals, Rotherham, in 1993, having been withdrawn after it fell into the turntable pit at Old Oak Common Depot.

No. 47649, 10 May 1986

No. 47649 (D1645, 47061, 47830) undergoes final testing before being released to traffic, having been converted from No. 47061. Today this loco carries the number 47830, and is operated by Freightliner, and has been repainted back into BR two-tone green livery.

No. 47654, 17 August 1986

No. 47654 (D1640, 47056, 47809, 47783) is seen ready to depart Crewe Works having been converted from No. 47056. At this time Crewe were outshopping additional ETH-fitted Class 47s for passenger workings. This loco was scrapped by Ron Hull, Rotherham, in 2007 carrying the number 47783.

No. 47655, 17 August 1986

No. 47655 (D1924, 47247, 47810) undergoes testing outside Crewe Works following conversion from No. 47247. The loco just needs a top coat of large logo livery before it is released back into traffic. Today this loco is operated by DRS and numbered 47810, but it is in storage at Eastleigh.

No. 47675, 10 July 1994

No. 47675 (D1969, 47268, 47595, 47791) is seen on display at Doncaster Works open day 1994 carrying InterCity Mainline livery. This had been renumbered from No. 47595 for Scottish sleeper trains, and carries the name *Confederation of British Industry*. It would go on to be renumbered 47791, and was scrapped by C. F. Booth, Rotherham, in 2013.

No. 47703, 14 September 1980

No. 47703 (D1960, 47514) *Saint Mungo* is seen at Crewe Works having received a new set of bogies. This was converted from No. 47514 for Scottish push/pull workings between Glasgow and Edinburgh. This loco is still in use today with Harry Needle.

No. 47703, 17 August 1986

No. 47703 (D1960, 47514) is seen undergoing testing outside the main repair shop at Crewe Works. It was always a highlight of a trip to Crewe to see some of the Scottish push/pull Class 47/7s as there always seemed to be one or two on Works at any one time. No. 47703 carries the name *Saint Mungo* and is waiting for the rest of its ScotRail livery to be applied.

No. 47706, 10 May 1986
No. 47706 (D1936, 47494) undergoes major overhaul inside Crewe Works. This loco had not long lost its *Strathclyde* nameplates. No. 47706 would be scrapped at Crewe Works in 1995 by private contractor.

No. 47706, 17 August 1986
No. 47706 (D1936, 47494) is seen on the arrival sidings at Crewe Works. This loco had already been through the Works for overhaul and had been out on a test run, that being the reason it had re-entered the Works. There always seemed to be a couple of the ScotRail Class 47/7s on Crewe at any given time.

No. 47708, 27 October 1984

No. 47708 (D1968, 47516) sits outside one of the test houses at Crewe Works following overhaul. This loco carries the name *Waverley*, and still sported an original headlight. At this time No. 47708 was the only Class 47/7 to carry ScotRail livery, being the first to do so. No. 47708 was scrapped at Crewe Works in 1995 by private contractor.

No. 47711, 23 May 1982

No. 47711 (D1941, 47498) *Greyfriars Bobby* is seen at Crewe Works, awaiting entry to the repair shed. At this time there were only two Class 47/7s carrying large logo livery – this and No. 47712. I always enjoyed seeing these Class 47/7s on Crewe, as they were very rare locomotives for us English-based enthusiasts to see. No. 47711 would eventually be scrapped at Toton by private contractor in 2004.

No. 47711, 17 August 1986

No. 47711 (D1941, 47498) is seen inside Crewe Works partway through an extensive overhaul. The level of work that Crewe put into their overhauls was impressive, and No. 47711 has already been partly repainted – note the chalk marks around the ScotRail branding to ensure the lettering is straight. No. 47711 carries the name *Greyfriars Bobby*.

No. 47713, 18 March 1990

No. 47713 (D1954, 47510) is seen on the scrap lines at Doncaster Works. This was withdrawn following fire damage, which can be seen on the side of the loco. This was eventually sold to Vic Berry, Leicester, and it was scrapped just four months later. When No. 47713 was withdrawn there was a need for an extra push/pull loco, and No. 47497 was converted to No. 47717 using many of the parts from No. 47713. This had once been named *Tayside Region*.

No. 47971, 21 May 2000

No. 47971 (D1616, 47480, 97480) is seen on display at Crewe Works open day 2000. No. 47971 had been used by the research department, and was one of six Class 47s renumbered into the 47/9 series for this work. By the time of the photograph this loco had been withdrawn, and it would be moved to European Metal Recycling, Kingsbury, to be scrapped in 2001.

No. 47974, 12 July 1992

No. 47974 (D1584, 47531, 47775) is seen inside Doncaster Works undergoing overhaul. When released from Doncaster, this loco would be renumbered as 47531 – indeed the number is chalked on the secondman's cabside – and it would carry RES livery. This was scrapped at Crewe TMD in 2006, carrying the number 47775.

No. D104, 18 June 1980
No. D1041 *Western Prince* stands outside Swindon Works, having been preserved. At this time there were a few former Western Region hydraulics at Swindon, but some were to move to Horwich for display at the open day in 1980, including D1041. Today this loco can be found at the East Lancashire Railway.

No. D1048, 8 February 1981
No. D1048 *Western Lady* is seen in storage at Horwich Works alongside D832. In the background can be seen a similar Western, D1041. These locomotives were in storage at Horwich, and had been put on display at the open day in August 1980.

No. 55003, 1 March 1981

No. 55003 (D9003) is seen as just a stripped shell in the scrap lines at Doncaster Works. This Deltic was originally named *Meld*, after the famous racehorse, and was but a memory by the month's end. These locos always looked better with the white cab surrounds.

No. 55014, 1 March 1981

No. 55014 (D9014) is seen at Doncaster Works. This loco was still in service at the time, but the whole class would be withdrawn by January 1982. No. 55014 carries the name *The Duke of Wellington's Regiment* and it would return to Doncaster for scrapping, which was completed in February 1982.

No. 55015, 15 May 1983

No. 55015 (D9015) is seen in the scrap lines at Doncaster Works, awaiting a decision on its future. No. 55015 would be lucky, and it was preserved, and today can be found at Barrow Hill. This loco was named *Tulyar*, and also carries the Finsbury Park-applied white window surrounds.

No. 55016, 15 May 1983

No. 55016 (D9016) stands derelict in the scrap lines at Doncaster Works. Doncaster used to scrap their redundant locomotives outside, unlike Crewe, but No. 55016 was lucky enough to find its way into preservation, and can today be found at Washwood Heath, Birmingham. No. 55016 was named *Gordon Highlander*.

No. 55022, 15 May 1983

No. 55022 (D9000) stands forlornly in the scrap lines at Doncaster Works. At this time, the whole of the class had been withdrawn, and just the last few survivors lingered at Doncaster, with No. 55022 being saved for preservation. No. 55022 was the original member of the class, and carried the name *Royal Scots Grey*.

No. 56016, 1 March 1981

No. 56016 stands in the yard at Doncaster Works. This was one of the Romanian-built Class 56s that struggled to enter service, and by this time had only been in traffic for four years. No. 56016 would eventually be scrapped at Cardiff Canton in 1997 by private contractor.

No. 56038, 17 August 1986

No. 56038 is seen partway through an overhaul at Crewe Works. The Class 56s were mainly overhauled at Doncaster, although Crewe did take on some of the overhauls at this time, having gained experience of the class when they built the last twenty members. No. 56038 carries the name *Western Mail* and would be released back to Cardiff Canton carrying a coat of Railfreight grey livery.

No. 56039, 10 July 1994

No. 56039 is seen on display at Doncaster Works open day 1994. This was one of the first locomotives to carry Loadhaul livery, and it was launched at this event. No. 56039 would be scrapped by T. J. Thomson, Stockton, in 2004.

No. 56042, 11 February 1984

No. 56042 is seen inside the main repair building at Derby Works. This locomotive was specially fitted with CP1 bogies as an evaluation for the Class 58 locomotives, and it carried them until withdrawal. This loco spent long periods out of use, and was eventually scrapped at Toton by private contractor in 1994.

No. 56051, 20 May 1990

No. 56051 stands on display at Doncaster Works open day 1990. This loco carries Railfreight Construction livery and displays a Westbury horse depot plaque. At this time the Class 56 fleet was more or less still at full strength, this would change significantly over the next ten years. No. 56051 is currently in storage at Washwood Heath, owned by Colas.

No. 56057, 17 August 1986

No. 56057 (56311) is seen on the departure roads at Crewe Works having been in for an overhaul. Crewe had not long started overhauling these locomotives, but they would only do a handful, with the majority being done at Doncaster. No. 56057 was eventually renumbered 56311, and is still in traffic today.

No. 56077, 20 May 1990

No. 56077 is seen inside Doncaster Works having been rubbed down ready for a repaint from original Railfreight to Railfreight Coal. This loco was named *Thorpe Marsh Power Station* upon release, and would go on to spend many years in derelict condition at Crewe Diesel Depot before moving to Leicester for safe storage.

No. 56081, 27 July 1980

No. 56081 is seen brand-new outside the test shop at Doncaster Works. This loco had yet to be released to traffic, this being done the following month. Doncaster built eighty-five of these locos before they started constructing the Class 58s. No. 56081 is still in traffic today, working for UK Rail Leasing, Leicester.

No. 56090, 1 March 1981

No. 56090 stands outside the test house at Doncaster Works. This loco had yet to enter traffic, and was one of the first handful of locomotives to carry large logo livery, with No. 56084 onwards carrying the livery. No. 56090 is still intact today, undergoing long-term restoration at Washwood Heath.

No. 56119, 2 April 1983

No. 56119 is seen brand-new at Crewe Works. Crewe took over the construction of the final twenty Class 56s from Doncaster due to the new Class 58 build. The Crewe built examples were instantly recognisable by having silver bodyside grills, compared to the blue Doncaster-built ones. No. 56119 would be scrapped in 2011 by European Metal Recycling, Attercliffe.

No. 56127, 29 October 1983

No. 56127 is seen inside the paint shop at Crewe Works, waiting for an application of large logo livery. It would be another three months before No. 56127 was accepted to traffic. This was another building that was anticipated during a visit to Crewe, as there was always a freshly painted loco on display. No. 56127 was scrapped by European Metal Recycling, Hartlepool, in 2010.

No. 56133, 2 June 1984

No. 56133 is seen on display at Crewe Works open day 1984. This loco had yet to enter traffic, and was named *Crewe Locomotive Works* at the event. The large logo livery really suited this class, and No. 56133 was scrapped by European Metal Recycling, Kingsbury, in 2012.

No. 56135, 27 October 1984

No. 56135 is seen outside the test house at Crewe Works before being released to traffic. This was the last member of the class to be built and was released carrying original Railfreight livery. No. 56135 spent most of its working life in the North East on coal workings and was scrapped at Immingham by private contractor in 2003.

Locomotives at BR Workshops 87

No. 60050, 10 July 1994

No. 60050 is seen on display at Doncaster Works open day 1994 carrying Loadhaul branding. This loco carries the name *Roseberry Topping*, and was one of one hundred built by Brush. Today No. 60050 is one of the many Class 60s in long-term storage at Toton, waiting a decision on its future.

No. 73133, 22 August 1987

No. 73133 (E6040) is seen inside Eastleigh Works undergoing overhaul, including a repaint into InterCity Mainline livery. Eastleigh undertook all the overhauls to the Electro-diesel fleets, as they were only used on the Southern Region. Today No. 73133 is owned by Transmart Trains, and is used as a shunter at Bournemouth Depot.

No. 74004, 3 April 1976

No. 74004 (E5000, E5024, E6104) stands in the sunshine outside Eastleigh Works following an overhaul. This loco started life as the original Class 71 loco E5000, and was rebuilt at Doncaster Works in 1968, emerging as a Class 74. No. 74004 would be scrapped by Birds, Long Marston, in 1978. No Class 74s survived, although Class 71 E5001 was preserved at the National Railway Museum, York.

No. 81001, 29 October 1983

No. 81001 (E3001) is seen at Crewe Works showing signs of fire damage. This damage would prove terminal, and the loco was condemned, being scrapped at Crewe in 1986. No. 81001 was the original AC electric loco, and was built by the Birmingham Railway & Carriage Company in 1959.

No. 81002, 29 October 1983

No. 81002 (E3003) stands on the reception roads at Crewe Works. Crewe undertook all the overhauls to the AC fleet throughout their lives, including rebuilds as well as classified overhauls. 81002 would go on to be the only Class 81 to be preserved, and can today be found at Barrow Hill.

No. 81015, 23 May 1982

No. 81015 (E3017) is seen on the reception roads at Crewe Works, having arrived for attention. At this time it was common to see both diesels and electrics on Crewe, as Crewe were responsible for the AC electric overhauls. No. 81015 looks good, still retaining its domino headcode, but it would be scrapped by MC Metals, Glasgow, in 1994.

No. 83009, 6 June 1981

No. 83009 (E3032) is seen on display at Crewe Works open day 1981. This locomotive was built by English Electric in 1960, and would eventually be scrapped by MC Metals, Glasgow, in 1993.

No. 84008, 6 June 1981

No. 84008 (E3043) is also seen on display at Crewe Works open day 1981. By this time, No. 84008 had already been withdrawn for a couple of years, but it would manage to linger in ever-deteriorating state at Crewe Works until 1988, when it was scrapped by a private contractor in the Works.

No. 85007, 25 February 1984

No. 85007 (E3062, 85112) is seen inside the repair shop at Crewe Works undergoing an overhaul. The work undertaken at Crewe was always very thorough, and indeed No. 85007 has had its bogies removed, and has had all its light bulbs removed as well. No. 85007 would be renumbered 85112, and was scrapped by MC Metals, Glasgow, in 1992.

No. 85008, 10 May 1986

No. 85008 (E3063) is seen at Crewe Works, having been through for overhaul. The loco looks spotless, having received a coat of BR blue livery, but it would be scrapped by MC Metals, Glasgow, in 1993.

No. 85027, 25 February 1984

No. 85027 (E3082) stands condemned inside one of the workshops at Crewe Works. This was one of the first Class 85 locomotives to be withdrawn following severe fire damage, as can be seen. No. 85027 was scrapped at Crewe Works in 1985.

No. 86010, 25 February 1984

No. 86010 (E3104, 86410, 86610) is seen having been stripped down for overhaul inside Crewe Works. The AC electrics were overhauled on one side of the main workshop, and the diesel locomotives on the other, but this was not always adhered to. No. 86010 is still in service today with Freightliner, though it now carries the number 86610.

No. 86316, 13 December 1986

No. 86316 (E3109, 86010, 86416) is seen inside Crewe Works undergoing major overhaul. When this was completed, No. 86316 would be released carrying the number 86416 and a coat of InterCity livery.

No. 86429, 14 February 1987

No. 86429 (E3200, 86029, 86329) is seen at Crewe Works having been involved in a serious collision at Colwich. The loco collided with classmate No. 86211, which can be seen behind. No passengers were killed in the accident, but Driver Goode in No. 86211 lost his life. Both locomotives were scrapped at Crewe in September 1987.

No. 87006, 2 June 1984

No. 87006 *City of Glasgow* is seen on display at Crewe Works open day 1984, carrying a one off special version of large logo livery. This livery was trialled on 87006, at the same time that InterCity livery was applied to No. 87012. No. 87006 was eventually repainted into InterCity livery, despite the fact the livery suited the loco well. This was one of the Class 87s that were exported to Bulgaria.

No. 87011, 3 September 1994

No. 87011 is seen outside the admin buildings at Springburn Works. This loco carries InterCity Swallow livery, and also the name *The Black Prince*. With the roof covered in tarpaulin, this would suggest that No. 87011 was in Works for transformer repairs. No. 87011 was not as fortunate as some of its classmates, and was scrapped by European Metal Recycling, Kingsbury, in 2011.

No. 89001, 17 August 1986
No. 89001 is seen under construction inside Crewe Works. This loco seemed to take forever to build, always being inside the Works. This was a one-off locomotive, and was eventually saved for preservation. The loco is seen nearly complete, just waiting for some glazing and a coat of InterCity livery.

No. 975813, 11 February 1984
No. 975813 (41002, 43001) is seen on the 'Klondyke' scrap lines at Derby Works. This former prototype HST power car had been withdrawn from service, along with its classmate, which can be seen parked in front. No. 975813 would be the unlucky one of the pair, as it was scrapped by C. F. Booth, Rotherham, in 1990, whereas No. 975812 was saved for preservation. A shame both power cars couldn't have been saved.